Costume in Context

Medieval Times

Jennifer Ruby

B.T. Batsford Ltd · London

Foreword

When studying costume it is important to understand the difference between fashion and costume. Fashion tends to predict the future – that is, what people *will* be wearing – and very fashionable clothes are usually worn only by people wealthy enough to afford them. For example, even today, the clothes that appear in fashionable magazines are not the same as those being worn by the majority of people in the street. Costume, on the other hand, represents what people are actually wearing at a given time, which may be quite different from what is termed 'fashionable' for their day.

Each book in this series is built round a fictitious family. By following the various members, sometimes over several generations – and the people with whom they come into contact – you will be able to see the major fashion developments of the period and compare the clothing and lifestyles of people from all walks of life. You will meet servants, soldiers, street-sellers and beggars as well as the very wealthy, and you will see how their different clothing reflects their particular occupations and circumstances.

Major social changes are mentioned in each period and you will see how clothing is adapted as people's needs and attitudes change. The date list will help you to understand more fully how historical events affect the clothes that people wear.

Many of the drawings in these books have been taken from contemporary paintings. During the course of your work perhaps you could visit some museums and art galleries yourself in order to learn more about the costumes of the period you are studying from the artists who painted at that time.

Acknowledgments

I would like to acknowledge the sources for the following drawings: page 6, foreground after D. Calthrop, background after illumination from the *Très Riches Heures de Jean Duc de Berry;* page 27 after Quennell. Colour pages: 'Norman Hunt' after Quennell; 'Women's Fashions 1150-1190' after N. Bradfield; 'A Carpenter' after Robert Campin.

© Jennifer Ruby 1989
First published 1989
Reprinted 1993, 1994

Typeset by Tek-Art Ltd, Kent
and printed in Great Britain
by The Bath Press
Avon
for the publishers
B.T. Batsford Ltd
4 Fitzhardinge Street
London W1H 0AH

ISBN 0 7134 6075 X

Contents

c. 1460

Date List

1066	Battle of Hastings, William the Conqueror becomes king. Loose, simple garments are worn by men and women.
1095-1100	The first Crusade. The Crusades continued until the end of the 13th century and had an important influence on fashion.
1186	Oxford University founded.
1200	Silks and cottons are being imported from the East.
1209	Cambridge University founded.
1215	King John signs the Magna Carta.
1294	The first complete Parliament.
c. 1325	The beginnings of tailoring. The silhouette is transformed as clothes are now made to fit the figure.
1337	Beginning of the Hundred Years War.
1348	First outbreak of the Black Death.
1360s	Expensive fabrics like velvet, brocade, silk etc. are being imported for the upper classes and beautifully woven fabrics are being produced in England due to an influx of Flemish weavers.
1363	Strict sumptuary laws passed, restricting expenditure on cloth.
1374	Great Plague epidemic.
1380s	Chaucer writing the *Canterbury Tales*.
1381	The Peasants' Revolt.
1390s	Fashions become very exaggerated. Pointed toes, costly materials and brilliant colours are popular.
1420s	Women's headdresses are becoming very wide.
1453	End of the Hundred Years War. English driven from France.
1455	The beginning of the Wars of the Roses.
1460	Women's headdresses are now very tall.
1476	William Caxton introduces printing into England.
1485	The battle of Bosworth. Henry Tudor becomes king.

c. 1480

Introduction

Many changes occurred in English society during the four centuries covered by this book. When the Normans invaded in 1066 and William the Conqueror took the English crown, Britain was a wild and untamed place, but by the time Henry Tudor became king in 1485, society had become more sophisticated and existed more along the lines we know today.

Medieval society was organized around the feudal system whereby everyone was protected by his lord and had to give service to him. The king was the most powerful lord in the land and also God's representative on earth. He owned all the land and gave some to his vassals (tenants-in-chief), who were the Barons, Bishops and Abbots. They paid for their estates by giving military service to the king and paying special dues. The vassals, in turn, gave land to the lords of the manors and small towns who had tenants of their own who could be yeomen, villeins or serfs. Everyone paid dues and gave service to their lord; everyone knew and accepted their place within the system and there was little movement between classes.

c. 1435

Gradually things began to change. The Crusades of the 11th-13th centuries were important as they opened up trade routes with the east and commerce began to expand. More significant perhaps was the fact that crude, loutish knights from Western Europe met with people from older, more civilized societies in the east who were vastly superior in learning and craftsmanship and the knights eventually returned bringing knew ideas and attitudes with them. Many people at home were inspired by the Crusades and went on pilgrimages. This meant that they travelled away from their homes which helped to broaden their experiences and horizons. In addition, more ordinary people were becoming educated. This was because many successful farmers and tradesmen earned enough money to send their sons to school and an education, combined with a profitable marriage, made it possible to rise up the social scale. In 1476 printing came to England and from this time onwards information and ideas spread more rapidly. All these changes were set against a backdrop of turbulence caused by wars, both at home and abroad, plagues and peasant revolts; all events which caused further movement of people. This meant that communications improved which, of course, influenced clothing.

c. 1440

The Normans did not bring any striking changes to English costume in 1066 except for their rather strange men's hairstyle which involved shaving the back of the head. However, by 1100 this style had all but disappeared and the Normans had adopted the English long, flowing locks. Loose, simple garments in plain woollen or linen materials were worn by men and women and cloaks, mantles, undertunics, underwear and hose were necessary for warmth in cold, draughty dwellings. The Crusades were an important influence on fashion as they made a considerable difference to the quality and variety of fabrics that were available. International contacts opened up trade routes and by 1200 beautiful silks and cottons were being imported

c. 1415

from the East to be made into fine clothes for the nobility. The Crusaders also returned from their travels with luxury costume accessories including silk footwear, leather purses and jewelled girdles.

Extreme simplicity characterized the shape of costume from the 11th to the 13th centuries and real changes in style did not occur until the first half of the 14th century when revolutionary ideas were introduced and the whole silhouette was transformed. Instead of being loose and flowing, garments were made to fit the figure, emphasizing the male and female shapes and tailoring began. These innovations were due in part to natural evolution but also to the stirring of the Renaissance in Italy. There, the human body was being studied and glorified in art and literature and tailored fashions helped to display the figure better. Brilliant colours, costly materials, fur and fur linings, patterning, motifs and jewelled embroideries were all popular, culminating in ostentatious displays during the reign of Richard II.

The new styles developed further in the 15th century with an even greater variety of designs and materials. There was great scope for display and extravagance which sometimes caused much inconvenience to the wearer, good examples being the exaggerated pointed toes of men's shoes and the large, unusual headdresses worn by the ladies.

By law, high fashion was defined as being the prerogative of the upper classes with diminishing privileges given to those in the middle and lower classes. This meant that wealthy middle-class people would not be allowed to wear clothes as sumptuous as those of the nobility. Sometimes royalty would hand down or bequeath garments to their servants but only after the costly trimmings had been removed. The recipients would later sell them to second-hand clothes dealers and eventually the same garments would be worn out on the backs of the poor. Clothes were a mark of status and it was possible to determine a person's rank by the length of his tunic or size of her headdress.

Fashion changes had little affect on the poor, however, and the practical, coarse linen and woollen garments worn by working people changed very little during Medieval times. Life was often harsh and priority had to be given to food, shelter and warmth so little attention was given to appearance. In addition, many people spent their entire lives close to their homes deep in the countryside, tied to their land and lord and would be totally unaware of changes occuring in the fashionable world of the rich.

In this book you will meet people from all walks of life and you can compare and contrast their clothes and lifestyles. You will see that at first fashions altered very little but as society expanded and became more fluid, clothing sytles changed more rapidly. Think about some of the points mentioned above as you read and look at the relationship between the changing society and changes in costume. This will help you to understand what it was like to live and work in Medieval Times.

A Nobleman, c. 1070

This is John, who is a rich nobleman. He fought bravely for William I during the invasion of England in 1066 and the king rewarded him by giving him control of two large estates in the North of England. John now lives on one of these estates in an enormous castle which he built for his wife, family and many servants.

He is wearing a tunic which has a wide neck, three-quarter-length sleeves and embroidered borders. The garment is very loose and is pouched over a belt at his waist. Underneath the tunic he has on a linen shirt and braies. These are loose, trouser-like garments which are held up by means of a cord running through the hem at the waist. Crossed linen bands keep them secured to his lower legs. His shoes are made of leather and are high-fitting to the ankes. His cloak is semi-circular in shape and is fastened over his right shoulder with a large brooch. In winter he wears a hood for extra warmth.

Norman men favoured a rather strange hairstyle at this time. It consisted of shaving the back of the head up to the ears and brushing the remaining hair forward onto the forehead. John likes this hairstyle as it is practical and easy when he is fighting or jousting and needs to wear his helmet.

John likes to go hunting and hawking in the extensive forests near his home. On the right you can see him mounted on his horse and holding his favourite hawk. He is wearing the alternative style of tunic which has long, fitted sleeves.

See if you can find out more about Norman pastimes. Who might have accompanied John when he went out hunting and hawking? What would they have been wearing?

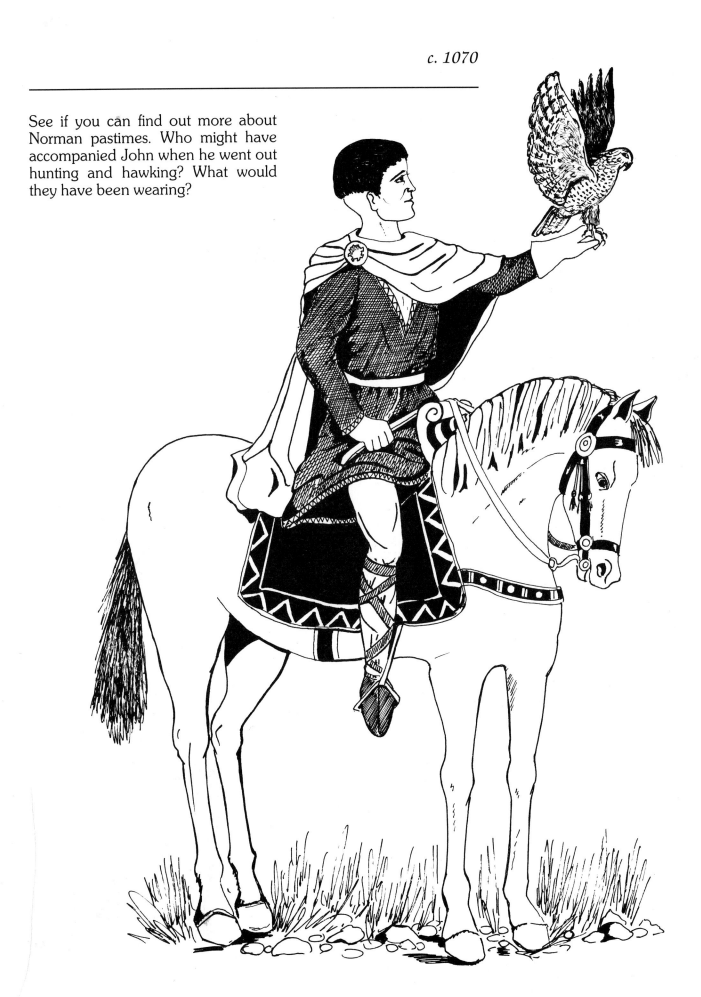

A Nobleman's Wife, c. 1070

This is Marguerite, John's wife. You can see from her garments that the dress of Norman ladies is quite simple. Plain woollen and linen cloths are used, relieved with a little embroidery. Marguerite's gown is similar in style to her husband's tunic, being very loose with an opening at the neck for her to put her head through. The neck, cuffs and hem of the gown have been embroidered and it is gathered into the waist with a girdle. Her head is covered with a veil which is wound around her neck so that none of her hair is visible. Over her gown she is wearing a voluminous woollen cloak for warmth.

On the opposite page you can see her in one of her other gowns which is slightly more fitted from the neck to the waist and longer in length. Marguerite always wears a chemise under her gowns which is a long, loose undergarment made of white linen. She also wears woollen hose which are gartered at the knee. Her shoes are made of leather.

John and Marguerite used to live in France before the invasion of England in 1066 and although Marguerite is kept very busy supervising the servants, planning menus, doing her embroidery and tapestry and seeing to her children, she misses her French home and the family she left behind there. What do you think it would have been like to travel across the channel and make a new home? What kind of dangers might travellers have encountered?

Adhêlhá

chemise

shoes

A Knight and his Lady, c. 1095

The Normans were very skilled at fighting on horseback and the knights were the most important part of their army. John and Marguerite's son Raoul is a knight. He has been trained in combat since boyhood and has fought in many battles.

Raoul is wearing a cone-shaped helmet and a hood of chain mail on his head. His coat of mail is called a hauberk. It has short sleeves so that he can bend his arms and is split back and front so that it can be worn on horseback. Raoul's hose are cross-gartered with leather thongs and he is wearing leather shoes on his feet. He is carrying his lance and helmet and his sword and mace are within easy reach.

Raoul's horse has been specially bred and is called a destrier. A destrier has to be very strong so that it can bear the weight of a knight and his armour and yet be able to move swiftly when necessary.

Raoul is preparing to go on a Crusade. He is being watched by his wife Matilda who will be sad when he leaves although she is becoming accustomed to his long absences from home.

You can see from Matilda's clothes that ladies' fashions have changed very little during the last 25 years. The only appreciable difference in the gown is that it is more fitted to the figure, an effect that is achieved by lacing down the back. The sleeves have also become longer from the elbow, a feature which will develop in later years.

Can you think of all the reasons why fashions changed so slowly during the early Middle Ages?

Find out more about the Crusades. What were the reasons behind them and who took part? Who were the Knights Templar and what was distinctive about their costumes?

13

Men's Fashions, 1150-1200

It is now 1150. Raoul's grandson Edward is a Duke and a trusted adviser to King Stephen. He and his wife have three large estates in the countryside but as Edward spends a lot of time with the king they frequently live at court in luxurious apartments provided for them.

Edward is wearing a long tunic which has a wide neck and sleeves with decorated borders. The skirt of the tunic is tucked up into his girdle at the sides, revealing his undertunic which is made of plain linen material. His hose are long and quite closely fitted with cross-bands up the leg. His shoes are made of leather although sometimes he wears hose with leather soles instead of shoes.

Towards the end of the twelfth century a new style of tunic made its appearance. It had unusual sleeves that were wide from the armpit but narrowed to the wrist and the long skirt was slit up the front.

Edward's grandson is wearing one of these new tunics on the opposite page. He also has on an ornate girdle and a full woollen cloak. His hat is called a Phrygian cap and is very popular with the wealthy. His shoes are fashionably low cut though sometimes he wears short boots like those in the picture.

When the knights returned from the first Crusade they brought exotic materials and new fashion ideas from the East. As trade routes opened rich people began to wear some of the new imported fabrics like beautiful silks and fine cottons and they adopted some Eastern ideas into their dress. Can you detect an Eastern influence in any of the clothes pictured here?

long hose with leather sole, crossed bands of leather over top

boots with coloured lining

15

Women's Fashions, 1150-1200

Here is Edward's wife Guinevere who is dressed in the fashionable clothes of the day. Gowns have changed little during the last 50 years except that the sleeves have now become very wide from the elbow. They are so cumbersome that Guinevere frequently knots hers up out of the way.

Guinevere is wearing a veil and coronet on her head and her hair is arranged in two long plaits which are bound with silk ribbon. The plaits are very long, reaching below her knees and she is very proud of the fact that it is all her own hair as many women use false hair to supplement their own thin locks.

Being a lady of rank, Guinevere wears special long girdles for State functions. In this picture she is wearing a long jewelled girdle which is high around her waist, crossed at the back and brought forward low onto her hips. The silk ends of the girdle are tied in front and have tassels at the end.

Underneath her gown she is wearing a fine linen undergarment which looks pleated. This effect is achieved by wringing the garment into a long twist when it is wet and then leaving it to dry.

When she goes out Guinevere sometimes wears a pelisse which is a three-quarter-length loose silk coat worn brooched at the waist. The pelisse is of Eastern origin and is very like the coats worn by Persian ladies.

The rest of the twelfth century saw little change in women's clothes except that long plaits and wide sleeves gradually went out of fashion.

In 1170 the barbette was introduced. This was a linen band that passed under the chin and over the head. In 1190 a linen covering for the throat appeared. It was called a wimple and was tucked into the dress at the front and often veiled the chin. Both these items became very popular and, after a few years' respite, ladies concealed their hair once again.

jewellery from the East

wimple (1190)

girdle

undergarment

barbette (1170)

pelisse

A Duke, c. 1260

We will now move forward to 1260. This is Lionel, a descendant of Edward and Guinevere. He is a rich and powerful Duke and lives partly at court and partly with his wife and family on his large estate in Yorkshire.

In the thirteenth century a new garment appeared called a supertunic, of which there were two types. The tabard variety was without sleeves and consisted of a long panel of material with a wide neck opening. The sides could be left open or sewn together at the hips. The other type was called a garde-corps. This was more like a long, very loose coat. It usually had wide tubular sleeves which were gathered in at the shoulders and it had a stand-up collar or a hood.

In the picture Lionel is wearing a garde-corps over his tunic. For convenience, a slit has been made in the armholes so that he can pass his arms through the voluminous sleeves. On the opposite page you can see the garde-corps from the rear, showing the sleeve and hood arrangement more clearly. Some of Lionel's shoes and a sword-belt are also pictured.

Lionel has his hair in the popular 'bob' style and is clean shaven. Sometimes he wears a coif which is a white linen undercap that he ties under his chin and on top of this he might wear a small round hat.

Some of his clothes have deep scallops cut into the hem. This is a new form of decoration and is called 'dagging'.

There was a much greater variety of materials available in the thirteenth century than there had been previously. This was partly due to the great trade fairs that had been established in Europe. Silks, satins, velvets and chiffon were available for those who could afford them and fur was more widely used. There was however, a definite hierarchy in the use of furs with coarser furs like badger, muskrat and cat being used by the lower classes while the pelts of finer and smaller creatures were only within reach of the very wealthy.

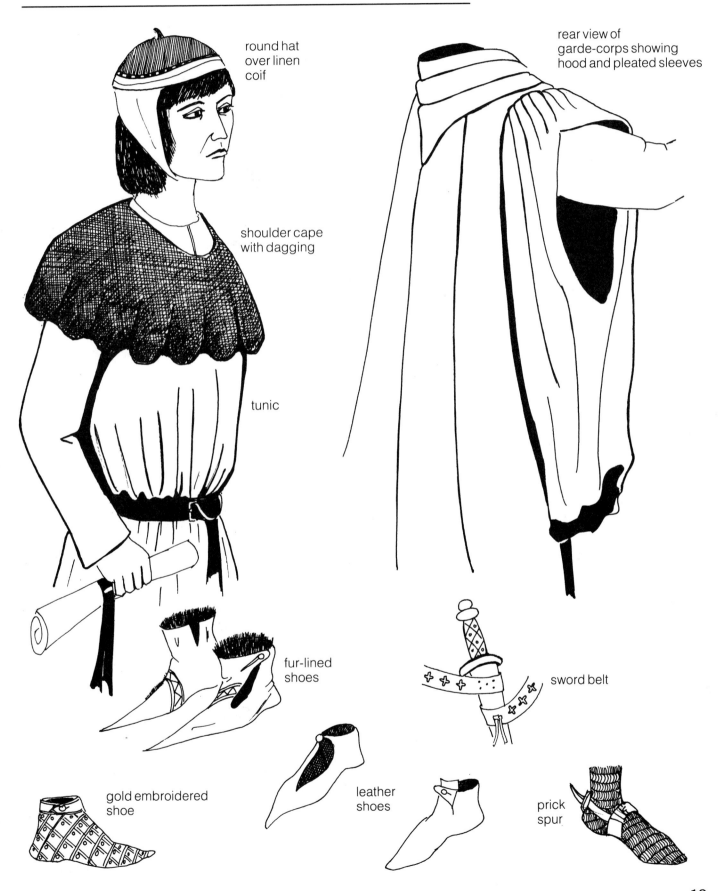

round hat
over linen
coif

rear view of
garde-corps showing
hood and pleated sleeves

shoulder cape
with dagging

tunic

fur-lined
shoes

sword belt

gold embroidered
shoe

leather
shoes

prick
spur

A Duke's Wife, c. 1260

Here is Lionel's wife Galiena. She is wearing a very long, loose gown that is so pouched up at the waist that her girdle is hidden. It has narrow fitted sleeves and an opening at the neck which is secured with a brooch. Galiena's hair is hidden by her headdress which consists of a barbette with a stiff band of linen, wider at the top than the bottom, on top. Her mantle is made of velvet and is lined with fur. She also has linen gloves which she likes to wear to protect her hands from sunburn.

On the right you can see Galiena with her new baby Edmund. She is wearing a simple gown and a wimple which is pinned to her hair above her ears. Edmund is in swaddling bands. (This was a custom that persisted for many centuries and involved wrapping a tiny baby in tight bandages to include its arms and feet. It was thought that this would enable the child to grow straight, protect it from harm and make it easier to carry!)

Other items from Galiena's wardrobe are also shown opposite. They include a different form of headdress called a crespinette. This is a coarse net made of silk or sometimes gold and is worn under a barbette and linen band.

What do you think an alms bag is for? Why might Galiena wear one?

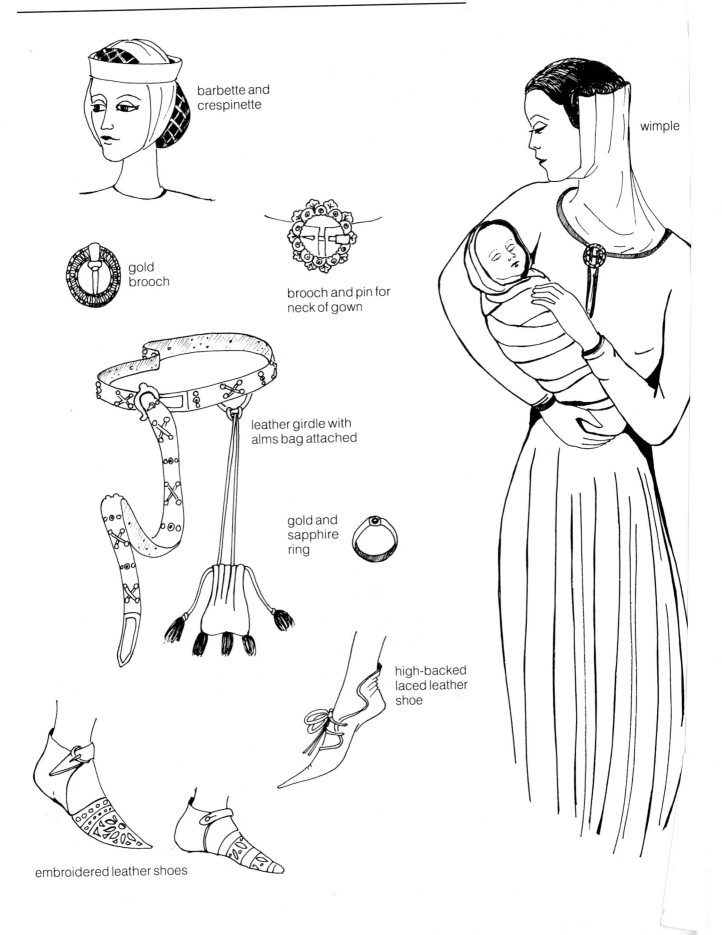

barbette and
crespinette

gold
brooch

brooch and pin for
neck of gown

wimple

leather girdle with
alms bag attached

gold and
sapphire
ring

high-backed
laced leather
shoe

embroidered leather shoes

Children's Clothes, c. 1260

Here are Lionel and Galiena's other children Mary, Eric, Roger and Philippa. It is the custom to dress children as miniature adults so their clothes echo the styles worn by their parents.

Mary is wearing a long sleeveless overtunic over her gown which has a V-neck and fitted sleeves. Her hair is loose and she wears a gold circlet around her head. Her doll is made of wood and is dressed in a similar style to her mistress.

The other children are enjoying a thirteenth-century game called 'hoodman blind'. One of the players is blinded by wearing his hood back to front while the others try to hit him with their hoods without being caught. Sometimes the liripipe (the tail hanging down the back of the hood) is knotted, but this makes the game rather rough. Hoodman blind was the forerunner of blindman's buff.

Can you find out more about the games enjoyed by children in the middle ages?

Philippa is wearing a similar outfit to Mary and the two boys are wearing belted, long-sleeved tunics, hose and short boots.

hood with liripipe

As Lionel's eldest son, Eric will eventually inherit his father's estate. For the other children however, the future is not so secure. Roger will probably enter the church and Mary and Philippa will have marriages arranged for them with suitably wealthy and influential partners. Young girls were often married at a very young age in the middle ages. It was not unheard of, for example, for a girl of seven to be married to a much older man. What do you think it would be like to have an arranged marriage? What would be the disadvantages of marrying so young?

Servants: Upper Ranks, c. 1260

Lionel and Galiena have many servants to look after them and ensure the smooth and efficient running of their castle. Some have more responsible positions than others, serving and waiting on the Duke's family. They are the 'upper servants' and rank higher than those who have more menial tasks like cleaning, gardening or working in the stables.

Margaret is the children's nurse. She is very close to the family and travels everywhere with them. She is well paid and wears fashionable clothes although not as sumptous as Galiena's. She is wearing a loose gown with a girdle at her waist and a veil which she has ingeniously knotted so that it serves both as a veil and wimple. She is talking to George who is a doctor.

George lives at the castle and is employed by the Duke to look after the health of the Duke's family and servants. He is wearing a supertunic with a stand-up collar and sleeves with vertical slits. Underneath this he is wearing a long, loose tunic with a round neck and long sleeves. His hair is cut in a fashionable bob and he wears a round cap. George is carrying a medicine box as he has just been to visit one of the kitchen boys who has a fever. Margaret is worried that is might be the plague but George has assured her that it is not. He has bled his patient and expects a full recovery.

Everyone feared the plague in Medieval times as it spread so rapidly and mercilessly. People had little idea how to prevent disease as they did not understand how germs multiplied and were passed on. There were few effective drugs and doctors used methods which, nowadays, seem quite strange and sometimes brutal.

Luke is the son of a prosperous vintner. He has been sent to the Duke's household as a page, where, in return for his services, he will be educated with the Duke's sons by the household priest. Luke is wearing a tunic bearing the Duke's badge, a hood with a liripipe, hose and short boots. He is carrying Lionel's 'tourney' helmet. This is very heavy and is not suitable for ordinary wear so is reserved for tournaments and great occasions.

Luke is only eight years old. Although he is quite happy in the Duke's service, he often misses his family. How do you think it would feel to be sent away from home as young as this?

Servants: Lower Ranks, c. 1260

Here is Martha who works as a maid in the castle. She is wearing a long-sleeved gown and has pinned the hem up while she is working, revealing her coarse linen undergarment beneath. On top of her gown she is wearing a supertunic with the full skirt hitched up on one side out of the way. Her hair is concealed in a piece of white linen which serves as a cap and she has leather shoes on her feet. Martha is taking a wine-jug to the kitchen for cleaning.

On the opposite page you can see Seth, a kitchen boy, who is working hard washing up some of the many jugs and bowls that have been used in the castle. The sink has an ingenious drain which runs through the wall to a spout outside. Seth is wearing only a tunic and as he is hot he has rolled up the sleeves and hitched up the skirt and tucked it into his belt.

Martha and Seth work long, hard hours in the castle, often getting up before dawn to begin their tasks after dark. However they are quite happy in their work. Both have many friends among the other servants and they consider themselves lucky to be receiving their meals and lodging in return for their services.

In the Fields, c. 1260

We will now move outside the castle walls and meet some of the people who live in the nearby village.

This is Seth's father Harry. He works hard all year round, tending his sheep, farming a few strips of land that he leases from the Duke and looking after the repair and maintenance of the simple home that he shares with his family. In addition to paying rent for his land, Harry also has to provide service to the Duke. This includes working two days a week in the Duke's fields, ploughing or harvesting or moving cartloads of produce. Harry does not have the time or money to think about fashionable clothes and his garments must be hard-wearing, practical and warm. He is wearing a fawn-coloured hood and shoulder cape, a rose-coloured belted tunic, blue hose and black boots. His hood has a liripipe at the back and is large enough to accommodate a hat for extra warmth if necessary.

Opposite you can see Will and Hal who are busy working in the Duke's fields. Will (foreground), is wearing a cape and hood with a liripipe, a belted tunic, braies and ankle boots. He has tied strips of grass around his knees and ankles in order to keep his braies from getting in the way and also to prevent mice from running up inside the legs.

Like Harry, Will leases a few strips of land from the Duke, but he does not own any animals. In addition, unlike Harry, he was not born a free man. This means that he cannot leave the Duke's estate, marry or inherit land without the Duke's permission. The only way he could obtain his freedom would be to run away to another parish and remain uncaptured for a year and a day, at which point he would be free from his bondage. Will has no wish to do this, however, as the Dukes rules justly and gives protection to his people.

Hal has been hired by the Duke's steward as a temporary labourer. He has no security and spends his life wandering the countryside looking for work. He is wearing a coif and a tunic with the skirt hitched up to reveal his hose which are made of leather. The difference between hose and braies was that hose were not joined at the top but were put on separately and kept up by being tied with strings to a belt around the waist. Braies were like loose trousers and were held up with a belt around the waist.

See if you can find out more about the feudal system in Medieval times.

A Peasant's Home, c. 1260

Here is Harry's wife Anne with their other children, Alison, Gilbert and baby John. As Harry owns a few animals as well as leasing his strips of land he is better off than many of the other peasants who live nearby. However, there is no room for luxuries and all clothes must be practical and warm.

Anne is wearing a coarse linen shawl which she has wrapped around her head and shoulders for protection against the wind, a loose woollen gown with a girdle, and a linen undergarment. She is holding baby John who has on a linen cap, woollen tunic and tiny leather boots. Alison, standing beside her mother, is wearing a hood with a liripipe and a long gown with a girdle at her waist.

Gilbert is inside their cottage where he is helping his mother by peeling vegetables. He is wearing a hood and cape, a belted tunic and ragged braies. Neither of the older children is wearing shoes.

Harry and Anne's cottage is made from a timber frame with walls of woven twigs coated with mud and clay. It has a thatched roof and only one room, in the centre of which all the cooking is done over a rather smoky fire. The whole family has to eat and sleep in this room and even their animals share it with them! The windows are very small so there is little light in the cottage. During the long winter evenings the family sit and talk around their glowing fire although this does not provide enough light to work by.

Try and imagine what it would be like to live in a house like this. What kind of constant smells and noises would there be?

Highway Robbers, c. 1260

Not far from the village the road skirts the edge of a dense forest that stretches for miles. Sometimes unfortunate travellers are attacked by gangs of brutal robbers who lie in wait for them among the trees.

Hal, who has grown weary of labouring, has now left the Duke's estate and has joined a gang of highway robbers. Here you can see them mercilessly attacking a lone traveller. The robbers are wearing belted tunics, ragged hose and short leather boots. Hal, in the background, is also wearing a hood and cape. Their unfortunate victim is a servant of Luke's father, the wine merchant. He has been travelling on business and has quite a lot of money with him. He is wearing a travelling cloak, a shoulder cape with dagged edges, a tunic, hose, ankle boots and leather gloves. He also had a travelling hat but that has been lost in the fray.

What kind of punishment would the robbers receive if they were caught?

Previous page: A Norman Hunt

Middle and working class,
c. 1250

Women's fashions,
1150-1190

Men's fashions,
c. 1350-1390

A carpenter, c. 1425

A knight, c. 1460

Court dress,
c. 1480

A Grey Friar, c. 1260

Further along the road from the highway robbery, we meet Thomas who is a Grey Friar. The Grey Friars were founded by St Francis of Assisi in 1212 and came to England during the thirteenth century. They were forbidden to own any property and begged food and shelter as they travelled from place to place mixing with people, caring for the poor and sick and preaching and teaching in streets and market places.

Thomas owns nothing but his grey robe as the Grey Friars believe that if the church is to help the poor then it must have men willing to share their poverty. His head is tonsured, which means that the crown of his head has been shaved, and he has no shoes.

The Grey Friars were enormously popular and their preaching helped and comforted thousands of people.

Men's Fashions, c. 1340-50

We will now move forward to 1340 and meet Richard, Lionel's grandson. He is very wealthy as he has inherited Lionel's estate in Yorkshire and has also been given two estates in the Midlands by King Edward III in return for his loyalty and service.

Great changes have taken place in fashionable clothing with a noticeable break from the traditions of the past. Garments are now made with a much closer fit, revealing the shape of the body, and men's clothes are becoming steadily shorter exposing the legs in tight-fitting hose. Buttons, which have previously only been decorative, are now widely used as practical fastenings.

Richard is wearing a cote-hardie which is an overgarment which in fashionable circles has replaced the supertunic. It has a low neck and is tight-fitting, with buttons down the front. The sleeves are tight to the elbow where they are finished with cuffs and long streamers called tippets. Over his cote-hardie Richard is wearing a hood and cape with dagged edging and a jewelled girdle at hip level. His hose are tight-fitting and have leather soles so he does not need to wear shoes. Richard's hair is cut in the fashionable bob shape and he has a small beard.

Over his shirt and underneath the cote-hardie, Richard is wearing a gipon (formerly the tunic). It fits tightly to his figure, is padded in the chest and is laced down the back although it could be fastened down the front in the same manner as the cote-hardie. The sleeves are tight, extending well over the wrist and are buttoned from the elbow. Gussets have been inserted under the arms so that he can move freely without tearing the material.

Shoes now have pointed or 'piked' toes, the point coming opposite the big toe. Some of Richard's shoes are pictured here along with other items from his wardrobe.

When Richard goes out he wears a semicircular cloak fastened on one shoulder. It is made of broadcloth and is lined with satin and with this he might wear a tall beaver hat. His wardrobe also contains many ornamental belts and embroidered gloves.

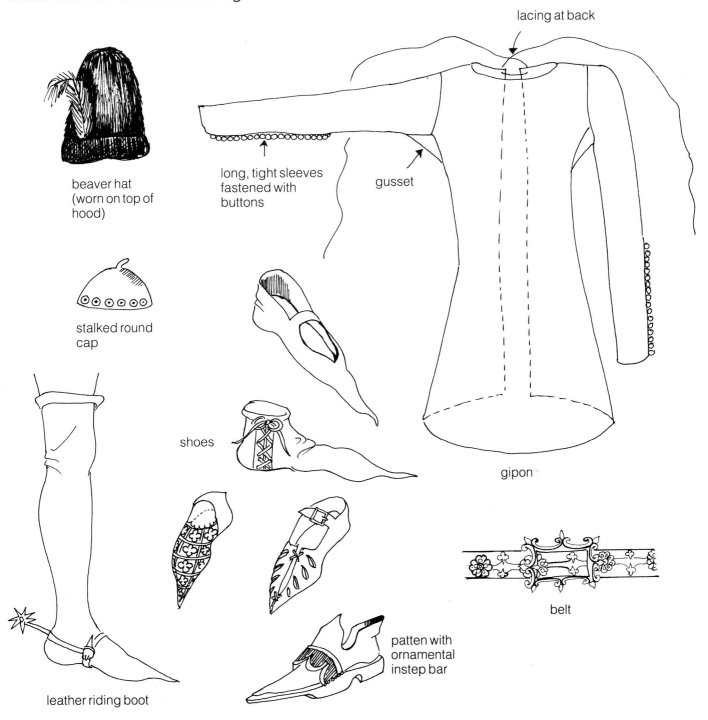

beaver hat
(worn on top of
hood)

lacing at back

long, tight sleeves
fastened with
buttons

gusset

stalked round
cap

shoes

gipon

belt

leather riding boot

patten with
ornamental
instep bar

Women's Fashions, c. 1340-50

Like men's clothes, women's garments are now more fitted to the figure, emphasizing the female shape. The long, well-fitted undertunic previously worn by women is now called a kirtle. It is worn over the smock and under the gown which, during this period is known as a cote-hardie.

Here is Richard's wife Letitia. She is dressed in the latest fashion which bears some resemblance to the men's styles. She is wearing a sideless surcoat which is a loose garment made without sleeves and has the sides slit open down to the hips. It is fairly fitted at the top and has a very full skirt. Underneath this she wears a kirtle with a low neck and tight-fitting sleeves which are buttoned from the elbow to the wrist. Her kirtle is very tight to the hips, has a full skirt and is fastened with lacings at the back. It has been beautifully embroidered by hand. Her hair is arranged in a large coil over each ear and she is wearing a veil and wimple. Letitia likes to wear jewellery and she has on several rings and a jewelled girdle.

On the opposite page you can see her in a cote-hardie. It is fitted to the hips and has button fastenings. Small vertical slits called fitchets have been made in the skirt front so that Letitia can reach her purse which hangs on her girdle underneath the cote-hardie. The sleeves are decorated with tippets. Another of her headdresses and some accessories are also pictured.

Contemporary reactions to the new fashions were not always favourable. One fourteenth-century writer objected to the new low neckline, commenting that it looked like 'the hole of a privy'!

hair in ornamental hollow pillars, veil hanging down from back

side view of left

tippet

gold ring with amethyst stone

fitchet

gold brooch set with rubies, sapphires and pearls

gold brooch set with emeralds and rubies

fourteenth-century embroidery patterns

cote-hardie

shoes

kirtle

Fashion and Sumptuary Laws, c. 1365

During the next 20 years the fashions shown on the previous four pages developed further, becoming more exaggerated, colourful and flamboyant. Parti-coloured clothes and long pointed shoes became popular and there was a greater variety of materials available. Expensive, rich fabrics like velvet, brocade, silk, and gold and silver cloth were imported for the upper classes and beautifully woven fabrics were being produced in England due to an influx of Flemish weavers who came to England under the patronage of Edward III.

What people wore was governed by their rank in society and as fashions became more extravagant, strict sumptuary laws were passed in an attempt to curb any excesses. For example, it was ordained that:

1) Only royalty and nobility could wear pearl embroidery and ermine.
2) Cloth of gold, jewels and miniver (plain white fur) linings could be worn only by knights and those of higher rank.
3) Cloth of silver, silver girdles and fine quality wool was restricted to squires and those of higher rank.
4) Commoners were permitted to wear only the coarser quality wools and even if they could afford jewels and silk they were not allowed to wear them.

What effect do you think these laws had on the structure of Medieval society?

This is James, Richard and Letitia's son, and his wife Isobel. Because of their high rank in society they are permitted to wear the latest fashions and most sumptuous materials.

James is wearing a parti-coloured cote-hardie with tippets over a tight fitting gipon. The cote-hardie is now much shorter, exposing his legs in tight-fitting hose. Hose are still made separately and are attached to the gipon by laces which are called points. They have leather soles and very long pointed toes. Over his cote-hardie James is wearing a shoulder cape with dagged edges and a jewelled girdle. His hair is cut in the popular bob style and he has a short beard.

Isobel is wearing a kirtle with front lacing, a low girdle and a long velvet cloak which is lined with embroidered silk. Her headdress is made from several semicircular pieces of fine linen, the straight edges of which have been pleated or ruffled together forming a frame for her face. This is called a goffered veil.

A Merchant and his Wife, c. 1365

When James and Isobel want new clothes they sometimes ask a cloth merchant to visit them with fabrics for them to look at. This is Humphrey who has travelled to London from his home in Suffolk to bring some materials for James and Isobel to inspect. He hopes to sell them some expensive cloth and has brought with him satin, silk, fine linen, woollen cloths and a new green Flemish cloth called siskin. Humphrey imports many of these fabrics from Europe and exports British wool to European weavers. He has grown quite rich on the profits of his business.

He is wearing a parti-coloured cote-hardie that is buttoned from the neck to the hem. It is knee-length rather than fashionably short as Humphrey is an older man and does not follow the latest fashions, although he could afford to. He is also wearing a hood and shoulder cape, parti-coloured hose and leather shoes. He is carrying a beaver hat and he has a money bag suspended from his leather belt.

Humphrey's wife Joan (opposite) has remained at home in their large house in Suffolk where she is looking after the household accounts, supervising the servants, keeping an eye on the family provisions and spending time with her children.

She is wearing a surcoat over a kirtle, a veil and wimple and leather shoes. Her hair is bound in two plaits and is arranged in large coils over her ears. The sleeves of her surcoat fit normally unlike the court ladies' surcoats which have the armholes cut so deeply that the front of the garment is a mere narrow strip. (Some churchmen call these armholes 'windows of hell'!) Joan's surcoat is made from woven silk that Humphrey has imported from Italy.

In the fourteenth century embroidery and woven patterns on materials were usually either geometric, heraldic or naturalistic in design. The pattern on Joan's surcoat is naturalistic; with intricately woven flowers, leaves and vines. Normally such beautiful fabric would be worn only by those of high rank. However sumptuary laws were difficult to enforce and people like Joan and her husband, who were affluent, tended to ignore them.

You can see another fourteenth century fabric design pictured below.

fourteenth-century fabric design

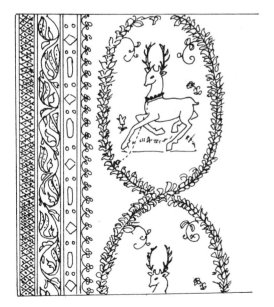

An International Fair, c. 1370

c. 1370

In Medieval times a fair was a great gathering of merchants and from time to time fairs were held in various parts of the country to which traders and merchants came from all over England and the Continent. One of the greatest fairs was held at Stourbridge near Cambridge and lasted for three weeks.

All the shops in the town were closed and the fairground was laid out in alleys of wooden booths and shops with each trade having its own street. All the local people came to watch and sometimes bought goods that they would never normally see in their town.

Humphrey is at Stourbridge fair with the cloth merchants. Look at the different clothes people are wearing and see what you can deduce about their lifestyles.

Pilgrims, c. 1370

On his way home from Stourbridge, Humphrey met a group of pilgrims journeying to Canterbury. They were a mixed bunch of people, travelling together for company and protection along the lonely and sometimes dangerous highway. Here are three of the party.

Clem is a miller. He is a rough but good-natured fellow and often entertains the other travellers with his bawdy tales and tunes on his bagpipes. He is wearing a knee-length cote-hardie over a gipon, a hood, woollen hose and leather boots. His hair is long and tangled and he has an unruly beard. The sleeves of his cote-hardie are old-fashioned as they end in the flap that has already developed into the tippet.

On the right you can see Elizabeth and Katherine, two more of the pilgrims. Elizabeth is a widow and and has undertaken the journey to Canterbury simply because she likes travelling. She is wearing a large travelling hat to protect her face from both sun and rain, a veil and a wimple. Her simple woollen gown is belted at the waist and has fur trimmings at the cuff. She is sitting astride her horse like a man and has tucked a mantel around her ample hips and over her legs for warmth and to protect her gown from the mud on the road.

Katherine is a sad figure. Recently her whole family caught the plague. Katherine and her two-year old daughter survived though her husband and son died. She is travelling to Canterbury to give thanks for their lives but also to pray for help for their uncertain future.

She is wearing a woollen shawl over her head and around her upper body. Underneath this she has on a simple linen gown. Her baby is wearing a hood and tunic. Both Katherine and her child have bare feet.

c. 1370

In the 1380s the poet Chaucer wrote his famous *Canterbury Tales* in which he painted a vivid picture of a group of pilgrims. Look at the descriptions of some of the characters in the Prologue to the tales and find out what they were wearing.

45

Men's Fashions, c. 1395

We will now move forward to the end of the fourteenth century and look at some of the fashion changes that are taking place.

A new, long, very full-skirted gown has been introduced, it is worn by both sexes and is called a houppelande. Its high neck reaches to the ears and is turned down at the edge so that it often looks like a ruff. It is buttoned from the chin to the chest. The sleeves hang very wide and long and frequently have dagged edges. The houppelande is made from four pieces of material with a seam at the front and back and one on each side. These seams are frequently left open for a short distance from the hem forming vents.

The cote-hardie has become very short and has the same neck and sleeves as the houppelande. Hose are very tight and reach the hips where they are attached to the gipon with points. The front fork to the hose is covered with a triangular piece called a cod-piece which is also attached with points.

This is Stephen, Richard's great grandson who lives mostly at the court of Richard II. He is wearing a short cote-hardie which is lined and trimmed with fur. Underneath this he has an embroidered gipon, parti-coloured hose and a cod-piece. The long pointed toes that we saw previously have now become very exaggerated and Stephen is wearing the points of his hose curled back and fastened to garters below his knees. Sometimes he wears pattens with his shoes to keep his feet clear of the mud and filth in the streets.

Opposite, he is wearing a houppelande, gaily decorated with dagged edging and a row of bells around the chest. His hat is called a chaperon and is simply the fashionable way of wearing the hood and liripipe. (The face opening is put on over the head and rolled back to form a brim, the shoulder cape then frames one side of the face and the liripipe hangs down on the other.)

Fashions are flamboyant, extravagant and colourful with folly bells, jewelled girdles, daggers and embroidered purses being popular accessories.

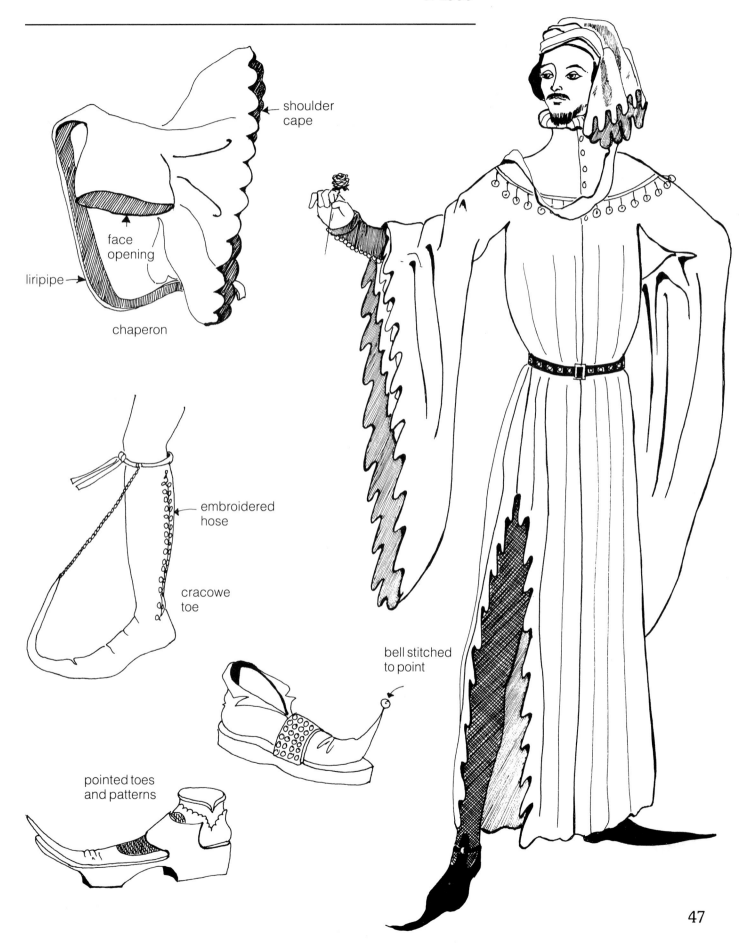

shoulder cape

face opening

liripipe

chaperon

embroidered hose

cracowe toe

bell stitched to point

pointed toes and patterns

Women's Fashions, c. 1395

This is Millicent, Stephen's fiancée. She is wearing a sideless surcoat which is made from fur and velvet and has a series of square jewelled brooches down the centre front. Underneath this she is wearing a kirtle with long tight sleeves and a jewelled girdle around her hips. On her head she is wearing a coronet and her hair is contained by a round headdress made from gold wire.

On the opposite page she is wearing a houppelande which is very similar in style to that worn by Stephen. It has a high neck, very long sleeves and is belted under the bustline. It is fashionable to wear a chaplet with the houppelande. This is a new form of headdress and is a wide, ornamented, padded roll made of silk or satin and is worn over the hair net. Millicent shaves her hairline in order to produce a high forehead so that no hair is visible at the front of her headdress.

One of Millicent's other gowns is also pictured opposite. It is parti-coloured and has a heraldic design woven into the material.

Fashions were very extravagant at this time. Women's gowns were extremely long and therefore used a great deal of costly materials such as silk, satin, taffeta or velvet. Garments were also brightly coloured in scarlets, blues, purples, greens and browns. Jewellery was very abundant. In 1362, William Langland wrote:

"I saw a woman . . . her head was adorned with so rich a crown that even the king had not a better. On all her fingers full richly she ringed."
from Piers Plowman

c. 1395

chaplet,
net and
veil

houppeland over
embroidered
kirtle

parti-coloured
heraldic
costume

Men's Fashions, c. 1420

We will now move forward to the fifteenth century and meet William, the grandson of Humphrey the merchant. William is very wealthy as he has inherited the land, property and business accumulated by his father and grandfather. He always wears fashionable clothes made from some of the beautiful materials that he trades in, like velvet, silk, satin and damask.

The most interesting change in fashion that has occurred since the late fourteenth century is the disappearance of the slim silhouette. The houppelande is very popular with both men and women and is made with many yards of material with sleeves and hemline frequently trailing on the ground. In the picture William is wearing a fur-lined, high-necked houppelande with dagged sleeves and hem. It is an extremely voluminous garment and William has to take care not totread on it whilst he is walking. On his head he is wearing a chaperon with a long liripipe.

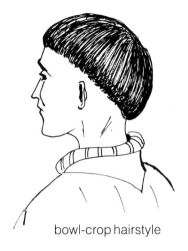

bowl-crop hairstyle

Underneath the houppelande he is wearing a doublet (formerly the gipon). It is tight-fitting and short, barely reaching his hips, and is laced down the front. His hose are joined at the fork rather than consisting of two separate legs, and they look rather like our modern tights. They only reach his hips where they are attached to his doublet with points. The points are made of leather and are tipped with ornamental metal tabs called aiglets. William is also wearing a cod-piece.

William has his hair cut in the popular 'bowl crop' and is clean shaven.

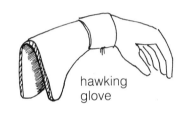

hawking glove

His accessories include daggers, pouches, jewelled girdles, gloves, scarves and walking sticks.

William is feeling very pleased as he has been approached by one of the great Dukes for his daughter Cecily's hand in marriage. William will provide Cecily with a handsome dowry and in return he will have the satisfaction of seeing his daughter among the highest nobles in the land which will bring prestige to him and his family.

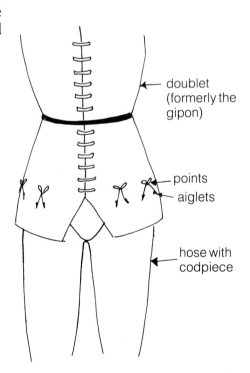

doublet (formerly the gipon)

points

aiglets

hose with codpiece

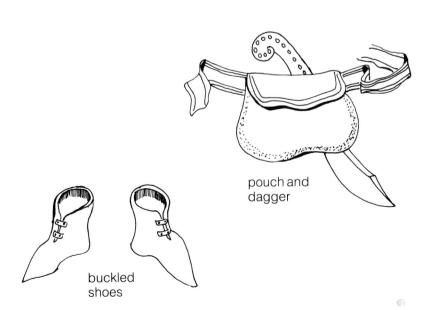

pouch and dagger

buckled shoes

Women's Fashions, c. 1420

One of the most interesting features of women's fashions during the fifteenth century was the variety and size of headdresses. For the first quarter of the century they were very wide, but gradually width gave way to height as we will see later.

This is Cecily, William's daughter. She is wearing a houppelande which has a flat linen collar instead of the high neckline that was previously fashionable.

The skirt and sleeves are so long that she has to hold them out of the way in order to walk safely. The houppelande is laced at the front and is belted under the bustline. Underneath this she is wearing a kirtle which is tight-fitting and has long sleeves which are laced from the elbow to the wrist. On her head she is wearing a large padded headdress in the 'turban' style, with a gauze veil.

On the opposite page Cecily is wearing other styles of headdress from the period. If you compare these styles to those pictured on pages 48 and 49, you will see how they have developed with the side projections becoming very wide, and the padded, ornamental roll increasing in size. The padding is usually dried plant stalks or other light material. When Cecily is married to the Duke her headdress will be very wide indeed because she will be a member of the nobility. She will also frequently wear a jewelled 'SS' collar signifying that she is a member of the great house of Lancaster.

One of Cecily's aunts is also pictured below. She is an elderly widow and although her headdress is not as ostentatious as Cecily's itis still a fashionable shape. As she is a widow she also wears a wimple.

top view of chaplet

'SS' collar

padded, ornamented headdresses with veils

headress worn by nobility

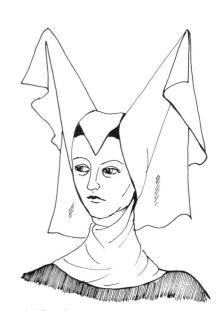

middle-class widow – linen head covering supported on wires, wimple

A Farewell, c. 1420

Cecily had to make a long journey from her Suffolk home to London where she married the Duke. The Duke sent a page and a large retinue to accompany her and when it was time for her to leave many of the servants and people who worked on her father's estate lined the route to bid her farewell.

Page: parti-coloured round felt hat, short cote-hardie, and hose

Nurse: cote-hardie with tippets, girdle and purse, veil and wimple

Child: long white gown

They included her old nurse, her younger brother and a farm labourer and his wife. Look at the clothes these characters are wearing and compare them with the fashionable clothes of 1420. Also, compare the garments of the farm labourer and his wife with those pictured on pages 28-31. Have they changed very much in 200 years?

Farm labourer: hood with shoulder cape (dagged edges), soft hat, tunic, cloak, hose, leggings and boots. Tool bag and leather pouch on girdle

Farm Labourer's Wife: hood with liripipe, laced three-quarter-length overgrown, kirtle, apron

Women's Fashions, c. 1460

It is now 1450 and the Wars of the Roses are in progress. This is Eleanor, Cecily's granddaughter who lives with her nobleman husband and their family on their estate in Wales.

As you can see from her outfit, the high neck and long, wide sleeves which characterized the houppelande have now disappeared and have been replaced by a low neck and tight-fitting sleeves.

Eleanor's gown has a tiny bodice with a V-shaped neck which is cut low enough to reveal her kirtle beneath. She also has a fine gauze scarf which helps to fill in the neckline. The gown is high-waisted and falls in voluminous folds with a train at the back. It is edged with fur and has a leaf pattern woven into the fabric.

Women's gowns vary very little and all the variety in fashion is in the different styles of headdress. Height is now the main objective and some of the styles are very tall indeed.

'butterfly' headdress

Eleanor is wearing a hennin. This is a cap made of velvet (though it could be brocade, gold or silver cloth), which has been stiffened into a conical shape and attached to a black velvet frontlet which is visible as a loop on her forehead. On top of the hennin she is wearing a fine gauze veil. Eleanor shaves her forehead so that no hair is visible at the edge of the headdress.

Sometimes she wears a butterfly headdress which is very popular and consists of a wire frame supporting a gauze veil which spreads out on either side of the head like butterfly wings, with a V-shaped dip over the forehead. On other occasions she might wear different styles like those pictured here.

transparent gauze veil low over forehead over cap of stiffened gold cloth

wired veil over jewelled caul

Men's Fashions, c. 1460

This is Eleanor's husband Clarence. He is wearing a jacket (formerly called the cote-hardie), which has a round neck and is edged with fur. The sleeves are gathered at the shoulder seam over mahoitres, or shoulder pads. Underneath this he is wearing a tight, padded and waisted doublet, the collar of which is visible at his neck. On his head he is wearing a chaperon which is now made in three separate parts which are sewn together, so it is now more like a hat than a hood (see opposite). Clarence's shoes are pointed and sometimes he wears pattens to keep them out of the mud.

On the opposite page you can see one of his gowns (formerly the houppelande), which is made of velvet and has fur trimmings. This one is floor-length although he has others which are calf-length. Clarence's page is also pictured. He is wearing a short jacket, chaperon, hose and pointed shoes.

These are difficult and uncertain times for Clarence and his family who are Lancastrians. Clarence has just been fighting at the battle of Northampton which was a victory for the Yorkists. Many of Clarence's soldiers were taken prisoner and massacred but Clarence managed to escape and has returned to his estate to rally more forces.

piked patten
with shoe

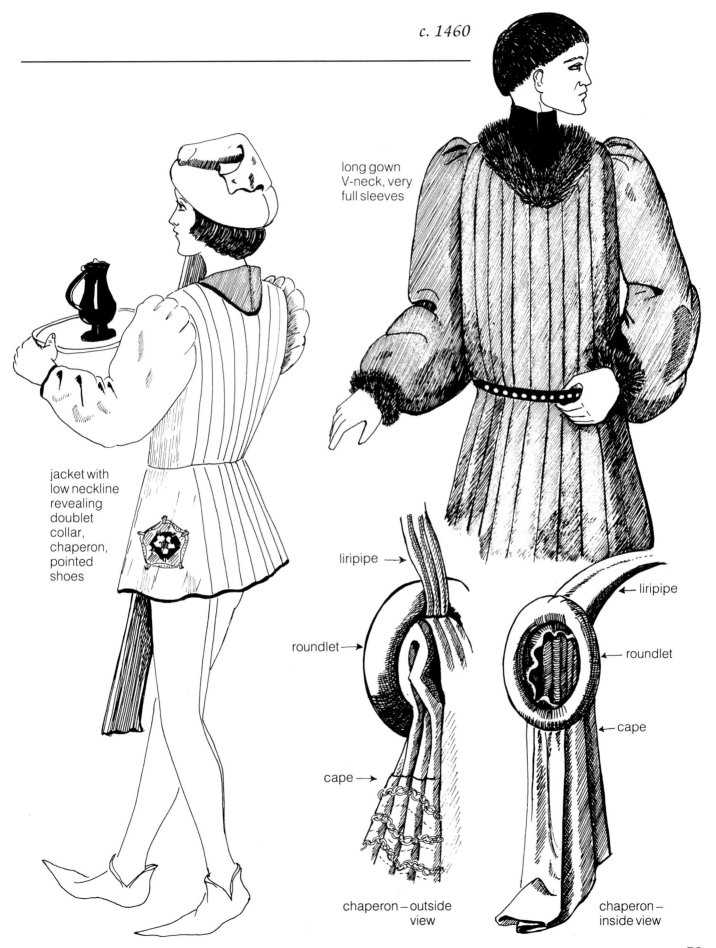

c. 1460

long gown
V-neck, very
full sleeves

jacket with
low neckline
revealing
doublet
collar,
chaperon,
pointed
shoes

liripipe

roundlet

cape

chaperon – outside
view

liripipe

roundlet

cape

chaperon –
inside view

Conclusion, c. 1483

It is now 1483 and we come to the end of the Medieval period. Richard III is king of England, but in two years time, Henry Tudor, the last of the Lancastrians, will defeat him at the battle of Bosworth and claim the throne, and then, by marrying Elizabeth of York, he will put an end to the Wars of the Roses at last.

Here are two of Clarence and Eleanor's children. Nicholas is wearing a short, black velvet doublet. The front is open almost to the waist and is laced across with satin ribbon. The sleeves are slashed between the elbow and wrist and tied at three places with silk. The lower portion of each sleeve is attached to the upper with points.

As shirts are now displayed more often they are finer in quality and Nicholas's is embroidered at the neck. His tights are long and he is wearing a cod-piece which is attached with points. He also has on a soft velvet cap decorated with a feather, a fur cloak, moderately pointed shoes and an ornamental silver garter. He carries a black velvet purse suspended from a belt and he is playing a lute.

Women's fashions have altered very little during the last 20 years and Agnes is wearing a very similar style of gown to that worn by her mother in 1460 (*see* page 56). It is made of crimson velvet and edged with white fur. It has a tight bodice and sleeves, a high waistline and an ample skirt which falls into a short train at the back.

Agnes is wearing the popular butterfly headdress and has a girdle at her waist and a jewelled necklace. Some of her beautiful rings are also pictured below.

Perhaps you would now like to compare these rich, sophisticated fashions with the simple styles worn by the ancestors of Nicholas and Agnes at the beginning of this book and think about how clothing has developed from the very simple, loose garments of the eleventh century. How do the developments in style reflect the changes that have taken place in society?

 silver gilt ring

 sapphire, gold ring

 gold ring

 gold enamelled ring

Glossary

aiglets	ornamental metal or jewel tags on the ends of points *(page 51)*
barbette	a linen band worn under the chin and over the head *(pages 17, 20, 21, 43)*
bowl crop	a man's short hairstyle, looking rather like a pudding basin *(pages 51, 59)*
braies	shapeless trouser-like garment, pulled in at the waist by a drawstring *(pages 8, 9, 29, 31)*
broadcloth	a type of woollen cotton cloth *(page 35)*
butterfly headdress	a wire frame supporting a gauze veil and spreading out above the head on each side like butterfly wings *(pages 57, 61)*
caul	a decorated net used in the headdresses of wealthy women *(page 57)*
chaperon	a hat made from the hood and liripipe *(pages 47, 50, 58, 59)*
chaplet	a wide, ornamented padded roll made of silk or satin *(pages 49, 53)*
cod-piece	the front flap forming a pouch at the fork of long hose *(pages 46, 51, 60)*
coif	a linen undercap tied under the chin *(pages 19, 29)*
cote	another word for tunic. A simple type of everyday dress worn by both sexes and all classes. The word cote (coat) did not begin to take on the modern meaning of an outer garment until the sixteenth century
cotehardie	a tight-fitting tunic when worn by men, a long, tight-fitting gown when worn by women *(pages 34, 37, 38, 40, 42, 43, 44, 46, 54)*
crespinette	a coarse net of silk or metal covering for the hair *(pages 21, 43)*
dagging	a form of decoration that involved cutting deep scallops into the hem of a garment *(pages 19, 34, 38, 40, 42, 50, 55)*
destrier	a horse specially bred for a knight *(page 12)*
doublet	a close-fitting body garment worn by men *(pages 51, 60)*
fitchets	small vertical slits in the front of a gown *(page 37)*
frontlet	the front section of a woman's headdress, usually a decorative band *(page 56)*
garde-corps	a voluminous garment with wide tubular sleeves *(pages 18, 19)*
goffered veil	a headdress made from fine linen with a ruffled front framing the face *(page 39)*
gipon	a well-tailored form of tunic worn over the shirt *(pages 35, 38, 44, 46)*
hauberk	a coat of chain mail worn by a knight *(page 12)*
hennin	a tall conical headdress made of cloth *(page 56)*
houppelande	a long, or short, full-skirted gown worn by men and women *(pages 47, 49, 50, 52)*
kirtle	an undertunic worn by women *(pages 36, 37, 39, 41, 43, 49, 52)*
liripipe	the long tail which developed at the back of the hood *(pages 22, 23, 28, 29, 30, 31, 32, 42, 43, 47, 50, 58, 59)*
mahoitres	shoulder pads *(pages 58, 59)*
parti-coloured	describes a garment which has the right half in one colour and the left in another *(pages 38, 40, 42, 43, 46, 49, 54)*
patten	overshoes consisting of wooden soles secured by leather straps and worn with boots or shoes to raise the wearer above the dirt when walking *(pages 35, 47, 59)*
pelisse	a three-quarter-length, loose silk coat *(page 17)*
phrygian cap	a style of round cap with a point at the top which was allowed to fall forwards *(page 15)*
piked shoes	shoes with long pointed toes *(pages 34, 35, 38, 46, 47, 59)*
points	laces used to fasten one garment to another *(pages 51, 60)*
slashing	cutting slits of varying lengths into a garment for decoration *(page 60)*
sumptuary laws	laws imposing restraint on luxury *(page 38)*
supertunic	a loose fitting garment with a wide neck opening and worn over the tunic *(pages 18, 24)*
surcoat	a long, loose overgarment without sleeves *(pages 36, 41, 48)*
swaddling	the custom of bandaging a new baby from head to toe in order to protect it and enable it to grow straight *(page 21)*
tippets	long streamers of material decorating the sleeve of the cote-hardie *(pages 34, 37, 38, 42, 43, 54)*
tonsure	the shaven crown of a monk's head *(page 33)*
tourney helmet	a decorative helmet which was very heavy and worn only for festive occasions *(page 25)*
wimple	a linen covering for the throat *(pages 17, 21, 24, 36, 37, 41, 43, 45, 53, 54)*

Book List

Birt, David	*The Medieval Village*, Longman, 1974
Black, J.A. & Garland, M.	*A History of Fashion*, 2nd ed., Orbis Publishing, 1980
Boucher, François	*A History of Costume in the West*, Thames and Hudson, 1987
Bradfield, Nancy	*900 Years of English Costume*, Peerage Books, 1987
Brooke, Iris	*English Costume of the Later Middle Ages*, Black, 1935
Calthrop, Dion Clayton	*English Costume*, Black, 1941
Chaucer, Geoffrey	*The Canterbury Tales*, Penguin, revised ed. 1958
Contini, Mila	*Fashion from Ancient Egypt to the Present Day*, Hamlyn, 1965
Cunnington, C.W. & P.	*Handbook of English Medieval Costume*, 2nd ed., Faber, 1969
Cunnington, C.W. & P.	*The History of Underclothes*, revised ed., Faber 1981
Cunnington, C.W. & Lucas, C.	*Occupational Costume in England*, Black, 1967
Cunnington, P.	*Costume of Household Servants from the Middle Ages to 1900*, Black, 1974
Cunnington, Phillis & Buck, Anne	*Children's Costume in England 1300-1900*, Black, 1965
De Marly, Diana	*Fashion for Men*, Batsford, 1985
Ewing, Elizabeth	*Fashion in Underwear*, Batsford, 1971
Ewing, Elizabeth	*History of Children's Costume*, Batsford, 1977
Hansen, H.H.	*Costume Cavalcade*, Methuen, 1972
Hartley, Dorothy	*Medieval Costume and Life*, Batsford, 1931
Holme, Bryan	*Medieval Pagent*, Thames and Hudson, 1987
Houston, Mary	*Medieval Costume in England and France*, Black 1939
Kelley, Francis M. & Schwabe Randolph	*A Short History of Costume and Armour 1066-1485*, Batsford, 1931
Laver, James	*Costume*, Cassell, 1963
Laver, James	*Costume and Fashion, a Concise History*, 2nd ed. Thames and Hudson, 1982
Lister, Margot	*Costume, an Illustrated Survey*, Herbert Jenkins, 1968
Price, Mary	*A Portrait of Britain in the Middle Ages*, Oxford, 1951
Quennell, Marjorie & C.H.B.	*A History of Everyday Things in England, 1066-1499*, 3rd ed., Batsford, 1938
Scott, Margaret	*A Visual History of Costume, the 14th and 15th Centuries*, Batsford, 1986
Unstead, R.J.	*The Medieval Scene*, Black, 1962
Wilson, Eunice	*A History of Shoe Fashion*, Pitman, 1974
Wright, Sylvia	*The Age of Chivalry, 1200-1400*, Kingfisher, 1987
Yarwood, D.	*Costume of the Western World*, Lutterworth Press, 1980
Yarwood, D.	*English Costume from the 2nd Century BC to the Present Day*, Batsford, 1979

Places to Visit

Here are some interesting places to visit to help you in your study of Medieval life and costume.

Museums   Many castles in England have museums with items from Medieval times on display. The Tower of London, for example, has a good collection.

Famous Sites   There are many Medieval castles, churches and cathedrals in Britain. Look at some of the old tombs in the churches and cathedrals to give you an idea of the kind of clothes people wore.

Pilgrims Way, Canterbury, Kent   Here, wax figures and audio visual techniques are used to bring *The Canterbury Tales* to life and give a good insight into Medieval times.

Yorvik Viking Centre, Coppergate, York   Here you can go on a journey back through time as far as Viking days. The Medieval times are included.

Things to Do

1. Look at some of the beautiful textile designs of Medieval times (eg. pages 41, 46, 49, 56, 57). Try designing a fabric suitable for a wealthy lady or gentleman in the fifteenth century. Look also at the work of William Morris (1834–96) and compare his textile designs with those of Medieval times.

2. Read about Highway Robbers once again on page 32. Find out more about Robin Hood and draw pictures of him and his band of men. Try to get their costumes as accurate as you can.

3. Find out more about Medieval sports and pastimes (eg. hunting, jousting). Draw pictures of participants in their correct costume.

4. With a few friends, try making a Medieval headress like those pictured on pages 53, 56, 57 or 61. Decorate it as colourfully as you can.

5. Look at the men's fashions on pages 46 and 47. Try making a pair of shoes with piked toes. What would it feel like to wear these all day?

6. Look at the prologue to Chaucer's *Canterbury Tales* and read the descriptions of some of the characters. Draw them in their costumes.

7. Find out more about these famous people: Joan of Arc (1412–31), Marco Polo (1254–1324), Geoffrey Chaucer (1340–1400) and William Caxton (1422–91). What kind of clothes would they have worn?

8. Look at the shield in the picture opposite. What do the words 'vous ou la mort' mean? Draw a picture of a lady watching her knight at a tournament or try designing a parade shield like this one.

9. Peasants often had a hard life in Medieval times. Find out about the two great plague epidemics and also the Peasants' Revolt of 1381. What kind of clothes would they have worn?

painted parade shield,
fifteenth century